UP!

How [...]
Aroun[...]
Carry[...] Little Ones

Written by **Susan Hughes** • Illustrated by **Ashley Barron**

Owlkids Books

From Ghana to Peru, from Egypt to Canada's Far North, from Korea to India, from Poland to China and Afghanistan and the place you call home, all around the world, families carry their babies in many different ways. Come join us and see…

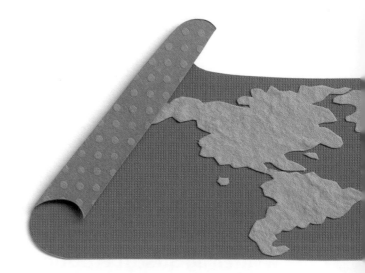

Upsy-daisy, baby—and away we go!

"Rise and shine, my little one.
Upsy-daisy!"

Baby cradled gently
in Mother's arms.

"Peek-a-boo, I see you!"

"Upsy-daisy, baby!"

Baby bundled snug-as-a-bug
in Sister's shawl.

"Upsy-daisy! Hang on tight!
Look, we're almost there!"

Baby *bouncy-bouncing*
on Brother's hip.

"Yes, my darling! Yes, my sweet!
Come with Granny, come.
Upsy-daisy, dear!"

Baby nestled safe and warm
in Grandmother's parka.

"Here we go, my bright-eyed boy.
Upsy-daisy!"

Baby comfy-cozy
in Father's carrier.

"A little tickle here.
A little tickle there!
Giggles all around, and … upsy-daisy!"

Baby cuddled close in Auntie's sling.

"We're off to the park to play—
and you're coming too, baby-o!
Ready, set ... upsy-daisy!"

Baby *jig-jogging, bip-bobbing*
in Cousin's pack.

"One twin in front, one twin behind!
Upsy-upsy-daisy!"

Two basketed babies seeing the world
from Uncle's shoulder pole.

"One yawn? Two?
Nap time for you, my sleepyhead ...
and an *uuuuuupsy-daisy*
to carry you off to bed!"

Baby hugged tight on Grandfather's
shoulders.

"And you? You too?
Do you want up?

All right, then!
Upsy-daisy, baby,
and away we go!"

To my parents, Iris and Raymond Hughes—with love,
now and always — S.H.

For caregivers everywhere — A.B.

Text © 2017 Susan Hughes
Illustrations © 2017 Ashley Barron

Owlkids Books acknowledges the financial support of the Canada Council for the Arts,
the Ontario Arts Council, the Government of Canada through the Canada Book Fund
(CBF) and the Government of Ontario through the Ontario Creates Book Initiative for
our publishing activities.

Published in Canada by
Owlkids Books Inc.
1 Eglinton Avenue East
Toronto, ON M4P 3A1

Published in the United States by
Owlkids Books Inc.
1700 Fourth Street
Berkeley, CA 94710

Cataloguing data available from Library and Archives Canada

Library of Congress Control Number: 2016946877

ISBN 978-1-77147-176-3 (hardback)

Edited by: Debbie Rogosin
Designed by: Barb Kelly

ONTARIO ARTS COUNCIL
CONSEIL DES ARTS DE L'ONTARIO
an Ontario government agency
un organisme du gouvernement de l'Ontario

Canada Council   Conseil des Arts
for the Arts   du Canada

Canada

Manufactured in Guangdong Province, Dongguan City, China, in September 2021,
by Toppan Leefung Packaging & Printing (Dongguan) Co., Ltd.
Job #BAYDC30/R4

E   F   G   H   I   J

MIX
Paper from
responsible sources
FSC® C104723

Publisher of Chirp, Chickadee and OWL
www.owlkidsbooks.com

Owlkids Books is a division of